The Chinese Language

Jennifer Lombardo

CRAZY
COOL
CHINA

ROSEN PUBLISHING

NEW YORK

华语教学出版社

BEIJING

Published in 2025 by The Rosen Publishing Group, Inc.
29 East 21st Street, New York, NY 10010

Jointly published in 2025 by Sinolingua Co.,Ltd., Beijing, China, and The Rosen Publishing Group, Inc., New York, New York, United States.

First Edition

Editor: Jennifer Lombardo
Designer: Rachel Rising

Photo credits: Cover, mauritius images GmbH / Alamy Stock Photo ; Cover, p.1, 3-48 Sylfida/Shutterstock.com; pp. 4, 6, 10, 14, 18, 22, 26, 30, 34, 38, 42 Anton Hlushchenko/Shutterstock.com; p. 5 testing/Shutterstock.com; p. 7 Bo1982/Shutterstock.com; p. 12 Giftography/Shutterstock.com; p. 15 Linaimages/Shutterstock.com; p. 19 Vietnam Stock Images/Shutterstock.com; p. 20 Pixel-Shot/Shutterstock.com; p. 23 yoshi0511/Shutterstock.com; p. 24 Dennis Gross/Shutterstock.com; p. 27 LeslieWang/Shutterstock.com; p. 28 Elena Shashkina /Shutterstock.com;p. 29 luchschenF/Shutterstock.com;p. 31 Andy.LIU/Shutterstock.com;p. 32 yul38885/Shutterstock.com; p. 35 Maria Passer/Shutterstock.com; p. 36 kerischeng/Shutterstock.com; p. 39 dongfang/Shutterstock.com; p. 40 badboydt7/Shutterstock.com; p. 43 aslysun/Shutterstock.com.

Some of the images in this book illustrate individuals who are models. The depictions do not imply actual situations or events.

Cataloging-in-Publication Data

Names: Lombardo, Jennifer.
Title: The Chinese language / Jennifer Lombardo.
Description: Buffalo, NY : Rosen Young Adult, 2025. | Series: Crazy cool China |
Includes glossary and index.
Identifiers: ISBN 9781499476156 (pbk.) | ISBN 9781499476163 (library bound) |
ISBN 9781499476170 (ebook)
Subjects: LCSH: Chinese language–Study and teaching. | Chinese language. | Chinese characters.
Classification: LCC PL1065.L66 2025 | DDC 495.107–dc23

Manufactured in the United States of America

CPSIA Compliance Information: Batch #CSRYA25. For further information, contact Rosen Publishing at 1-800-237-9932.

Find us on

Contents

Understanding Chinese

Chinese is a **unique** and **complex** language. In fact, it's not just one language at all. "Chinese" refers to a group of related languages. The two best-known of these are Mandarin and Cantonese. However, Chinese includes at least 300 spoken languages. Most of these are thousands of years old, making Chinese one of the world's oldest continuously spoken languages.

There's an important difference between "oldest language" and "oldest continuously spoken language." Languages such as Egyptian, Latin, and Sumerian are much older than Chinese. However, those are dead languages, meaning they have no native speakers anymore.

Chinese is also one of the most commonly spoken languages in the world. About 1.3 billion people speak at least one of the Chinese languages as their native language. That's about 16 percent of the world's population.

In the 1930s, China made Standard Chinese its official language. An official language is used by the government and taught in schools. Standard Chinese is a form of Mandarin, which is the most commonly spoken Chinese language. About 70 percent of Chinese speak at least one **dialect** of Mandarin.

As of 2024, China is the most populous country on Earth. Not everyone who speaks Chinese lives in China.

A Tonal Language

Most of the Chinese languages are tonal. Mandarin has four tones, which are numbered. Tone 1 is flat and has a higher pitch. Tone 2 is rising; it starts neutral and ends a little higher, like someone asking a question in English. Tone 3 is a falling/rising tone. It starts mid-low, dips very low, then rises high. Tone 4 is falling, starting high and quickly falling to low. Other Chinese languages may have more or fewer tones.

Some people say Mandarin has five tones. The fifth tone is neutral, meaning there is no tone change at all. It's different than Tone 1 because it is pitched lower.

In a tonal language, how a word is said determines its meaning. For example, in Mandarin, the word *ma* said in Tone 1 means "mother." Spoken in Tone 3, it means "horse." In a non-tonal language such as English, this is not the case. "Bat" is pronounced the same way whether a person is talking about a flying animal or a wooden stick used to hit a ball in baseball.

When a person speaks Chinese fluently, or very well, they can use the right tone at the right time without thinking too hard about it.

This picture shows how the tones are spoken. The third line here indicates a normal speaking voice. For example, when someone uses Tone 1, they start out higher than normal.

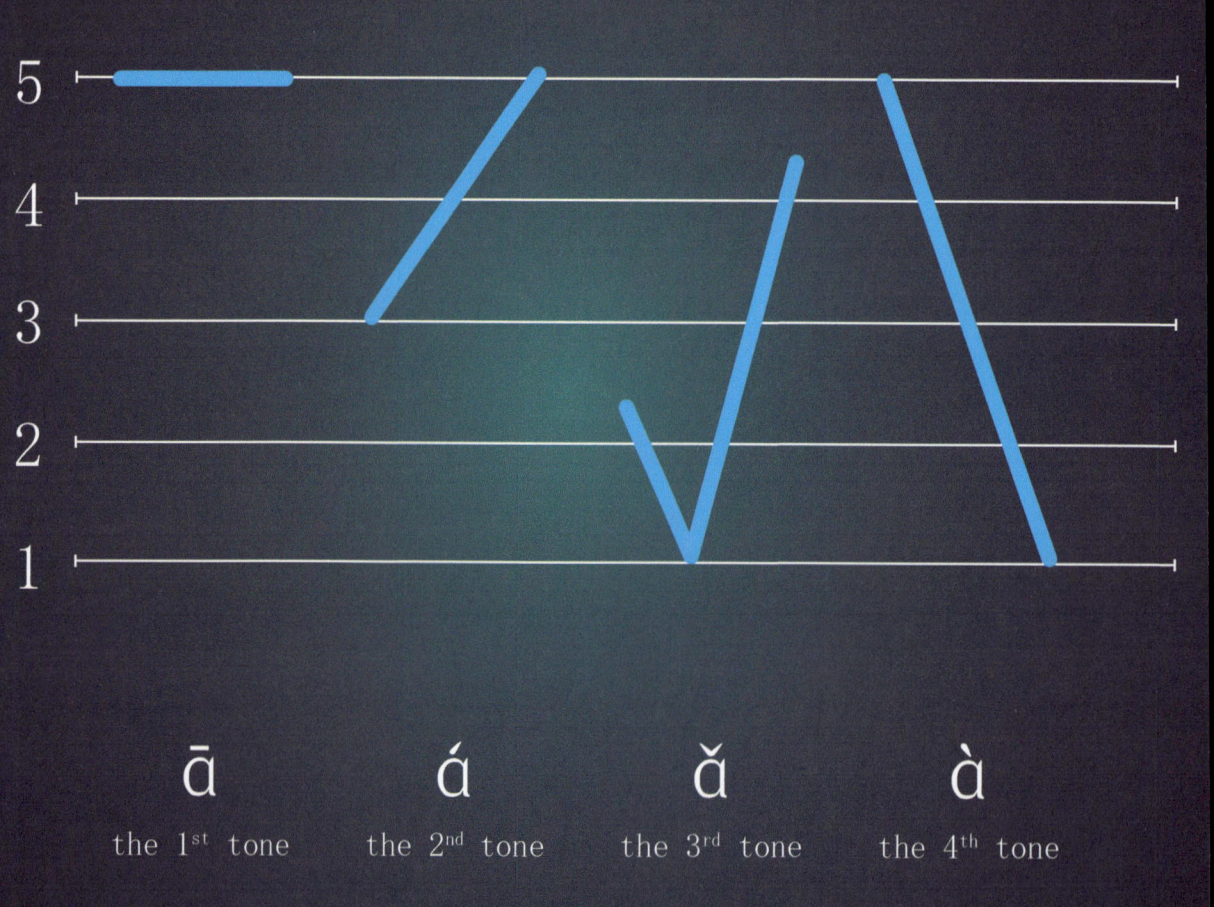

ā
the 1st tone

á
the 2nd tone

ǎ
the 3rd tone

à
the 4th tone

Many African and Asian languages are tonal. Most other languages are non-tonal. Chinese has greatly influenced other East Asian languages, such as Vietnamese, Korean, and Japanese.

There are three important aspects of spoken language: tone, pitch, and stress. The tones in Chinese are determined by the pitch of the speaker's voice. The overall tone of a sentence refers to the attitude in which it is spoken. For example, a person can have an angry or happy tone. This kind of tone is not the same as the tones in a tonal language. Stress is the emphasis a person puts on certain words. In English, this stress can change the meaning of a sentence. For example, "*You* are going to be late" indicates that only the person who is being spoken to will be late, while "You *are* going to be late" indicates that the person being spoken to falsely believes they will not be late. In Chinese, stress does not matter as much to the sentence's meaning as pitch and tone.

Chinese Writing

Although many different Chinese languages exist, there is only one written language. This helps unite all Chinese speakers; even if they can't understand each other's speech, they can understand each other by writing down what they want to say.

The written Chinese language is logographic. This means that it uses pictures called characters, or *hanzi*, to stand for meanings. The ways these characters are combined determine the meaning of a word or sentence. Learning the Chinese writing system can be challenging because there are thousands of characters to memorize, unlike the English alphabet, which has only 26 letters to memorize.

The oldest languages in the world, including Egyptian hieroglyphs and Sumerian cuneiform, are logographic. Chinese is the only logographic language still in use today. Most written languages in use today are alphabetical, which means they use symbols that stand for certain sounds.

山
shān
mountain

峰
fēng
peak

岩
yán
cliff

岛
dǎo
island

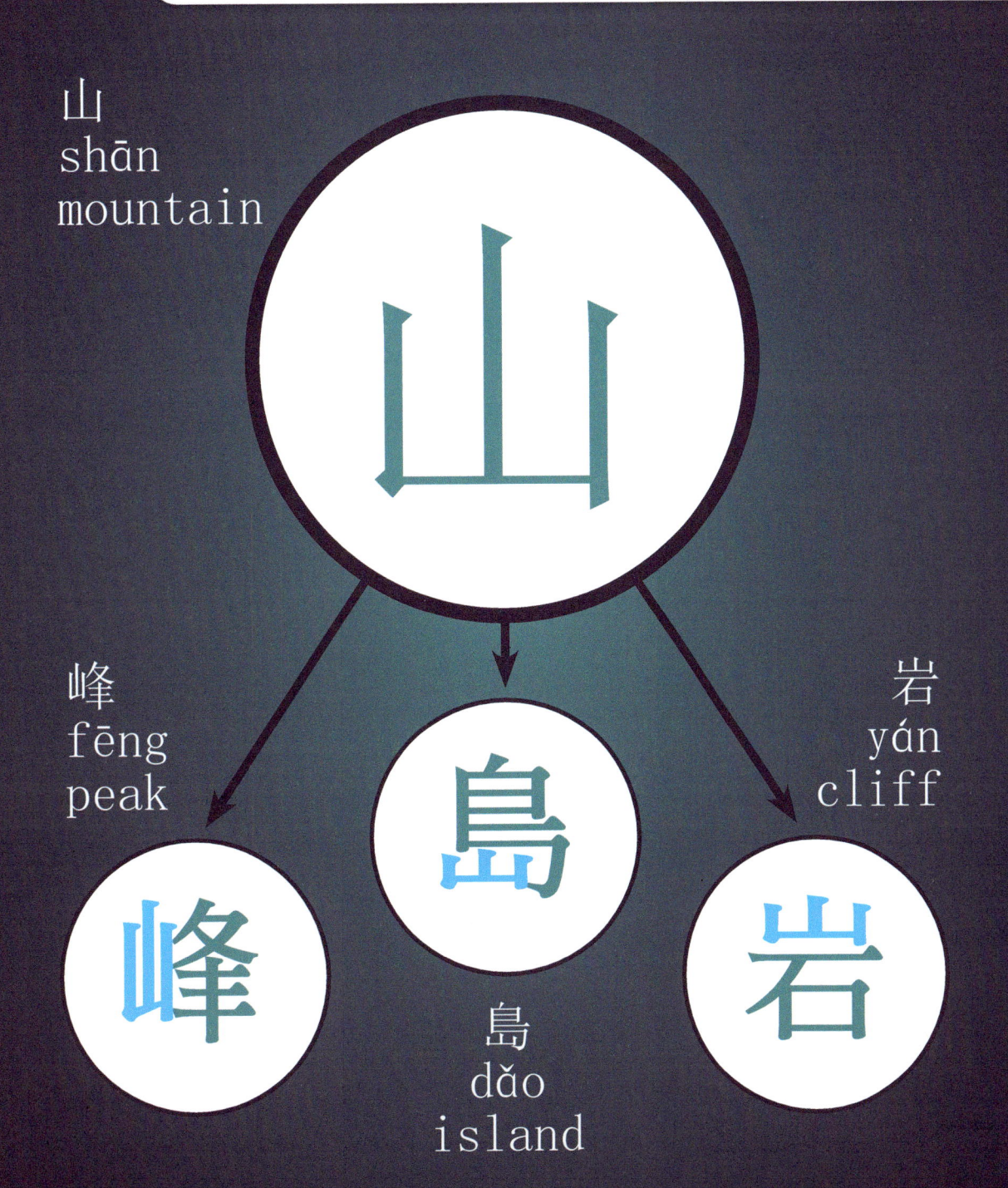

Something as simple as reading a newspaper requires knowing thousands of characters.

Most other languages, including English, have homophones as well. However, these other languages tend to have far fewer homophones than Chinese, and it is generally easy to figure out their meaning from **context**.

A person who speaks English and knows the letters of the English alphabet can read and understand most English words, even if they don't know how to pronounce them correctly. However, because Chinese characters don't **correspond** to sounds, learning how to read Chinese without knowing how to speak the language is possible.

Hanzi suits the Chinese language better than an alphabet would because there are hundreds of **homophones** in Chinese. These words have the exact same pronunciation, including tone, which makes it hard to tell what the word is supposed to be. For example, the words "reward" and "revenge" sound the same in Chinese. If they were written the same way, it would be impossible to tell the meanings apart. However, because they have different characters, the meanings are clear when they are written.

Traditional vs. Simplified

Written Chinese is even more complex than it seems on the surface because there are multiple different forms of the written language. Traditional Chinese is the oldest form of the Chinese writing system. It uses complex characters that can be difficult to memorize and write correctly. These characters are made up of many different lines, each one of which is added with the stroke of a pen or inked brush. One stroke in the wrong place can completely change the meaning of a written word.

When the People's Republic of China was founded in 1949, the literacy rate, or the number of people who could read, was very low. To make it easier for Chinese

Simplified Chinese is more commonly used by Chinese speakers in the Chinese mainland, Malaysia, and Singapore. Traditional Chinese is still widely used in places that favor Cantonese, such as Hong Kong and Macao. It's also more commonly used by Chinese living in other countries.

people to learn how to read, the government made the writing system simpler. This form, understandably called simplified Chinese, combined many of the traditional characters into forms that were easier to recognize and write correctly. Simplified characters have fewer strokes, and the same character can mean more than one thing. In contrast, each character in traditional Chinese means something different.

This picture shows flash cards. Each one has a picture on top. The name of each thing pictured is written below in English, *hanzi*, and pinyin.

These pictures show some examples of the differences between the simplified and traditional characters for a single word.

Book

simplified

traditional

书

書

Meal

simplified

traditional

Tone 1 in pinyin is indicated with a straight line over the letter (ā). Tone 2 is indicated with a right-leaning accent mark (á). Tone 3 is indicated with an **inverted** caret (ǎ). Tone 4 is indicated with a left-leaning accent mark (à). If there is no accent mark at all, the tone is neutral.

Another form of Chinese writing that is commonly used is called pinyin. This form of writing uses the Latin alphabet—the same one the English written language uses. The different tones are indicated with different accent marks. Pinyin can be helpful in some situations, but it isn't a good replacement for the entire Chinese logographic writing system. This is because Chinese homophones are written exactly the same way in pinyin. Compare "reward" (报酬, bào chóu) with "revenge" (报仇, bào chóu). The difference is only clear when the words are written in *hanzi*.

Cat

simplified

猫

traditional

貓

Calligraphy

Calligraphy is an artistic form of writing. Any language can be written in calligraphy. However, in China, calligraphy is a very important art form that has been practiced for centuries.

Just as English can be written in many different **fonts** and handwriting styles, *hanzi* can be written in many different ways that can all be considered correct. "Regular script" is the name for the official versions of *hanzi* characters. The Chinese government uses regular script in documents, signs, and other written materials. *Hanzi* can be handwritten with a pen or pencil, or it can be typed on a computer that has the right keyboard and software.

China was the first known country in the world to create civil service exams. A civil service exam is a test a person takes to prove that they are a good candidate for a government job. Between the early 600s and 1905, the Chinese civil service exams included a test of how well a person could write in regular script.

Calligraphers can choose from many different brush sizes to make their art.

19

Chinese characters work well with the calligraphy art form.

In artistic works, such as handwritten books and paintings, artists often write *hanzi* in calligraphy. A calligrapher uses four tools: a brush; silk, paper, wood, or another material for writing on; ink, which comes in a solid stick; and an inkstone. The calligrapher places a small amount of water onto the inkstone and then grinds the inkstick into it. This creates a liquid ink. The calligrapher uses the brush like a pen, dipping it into the ink and writing on the paper or other material.

In China, calligraphy is one of the most beautiful and beloved art forms. Although it might seem easy to do, it actually requires years of study and practice. A calligrapher must pay attention to things such as the spacing between the strokes as well as the size and shape of the strokes. They must create a beautiful work of art that is not too **abstract** to read. Since ink cannot be erased, they must also learn how to do this without making mistakes.

Chinese Around the World

China is an ancient country, and it has had many years to influence other Asian countries. Due to trade and travel, Chinese

"Sino" is a word that means "relating to China." For example, a Vietnamese word that comes from Chinese is called a Sino-Vietnamese word.

languages spread to countries such as Vietnam, Korea, Japan, Singapore, Malaysia, Indonesia, and more. These countries already had their own languages, so they generally did not completely adopt Chinese. They did add many Chinese words to their vocabulary, but they generally pronounced them according to the rules of their native language. Many countries also wrote their own language in *hanzi*.

For hundreds of years, only the wealthiest families in most Asian countries could afford to send their children to school, where they learned how to write *hanzi*. When countries such as Japan, South Korea, and Vietnam began creating simpler writing systems that were easier for people to learn, knowing the more complex *hanzi* became a sign of intelligence and wealth.

Japanese kanji looks very similar to Chinese *hanzi*.

氣 元 之 家 國 才 賢

HIỀN TÀI LÀ NGUYÊN KHÍ CỦA QUỐC GIA

This sign in a Vietnamese temple has the same sentence written in both chữ nôm and quốc ngữ.

As of 2024, Cantonese is an official language in two places: Hong Kong and Macao.

In some areas, it's still very easy to see the Chinese influence on other languages. For example, Japanese writing, which is called kanji, is very similar to *hanzi*. However, because kanji represents the Japanese language, the pronunciations of the characters are often very different. The same is true of Korean writing. Korean that is written with Chinese characters is called *hanja*. However, most Koreans today write in a script called hangul.

The Vietnamese **imperial** court used a form of writing called chữ nho until about the 13th century. Chữ nho was based on *hanzi*. Over time, scholars and the ruling class changed the script so that it was less logographic and more phonetic, or based on sounds instead of ideas. This new writing style was known as chữ nôm. Today, chữ nôm is only used for artistic purposes. In daily life, Vietnamese use a Latinized form of their alphabet called *quốc ngữ*.

Exchanging Words

Words that are added to one language from another are called loanwords. Thanks to the ease of travel in the 20th and 21st centuries, most languages today have loanwords from multiple different languages. For example, English has "banana" from Spanish, "cruise" from Dutch, "tsunami" from Japanese, and "pajamas" from Hindi. English also has some Chinese loanwords. These are mainly words for food, such as "dim sum" and "tea," as well as fighting styles such as "kung fu" and "tai chi."

About 80 percent of the English language is made up of loanwords from more than 350 different languages. Compared to English, Chinese has very few loanwords.

Chinese has very few loanwords overall. Over time, as the world grew more connected, China began to borrow certain words for things that were not already named in Chinese. From Sanskrit, an ancient Indian language, Mandarin Chinese took words meaning "apple," "instant," and things relating to Buddhism. From Persian, another ancient language spoken mainly in the Middle East and Central Asia, Chinese added words meaning "almond," "grape," "lion," and "bazaar," or marketplace.

China was the first country in history to brew tea.

Muffins are not a traditional Chinese food, so Chinese did not have a word for muffins until they arrived in the country. It made the most sense to use the name the food already had rather than inventing a new one.

The ancient country of Persia is today known as Iran. In the past, trade between Persia and China was very important to both countries, leading to language exchange as well.

By far, most of Chinese's loanwords come from English. Sometimes these words are pronounced almost exactly the same way they are in English. For instance, "mini," meaning "small," is "mínǐ" in pinyin. "Muffin" is "mǎfēn," and "penicillin" is "pánníxīlín" (the x makes a "sh" sound in Mandarin). Other words are changed a little more to make them easier to say in Chinese. These include "rum" (lǎngmǔjiǔ), "carnival" (jiāniánhuá), and "mug" (mǎkèbēi).

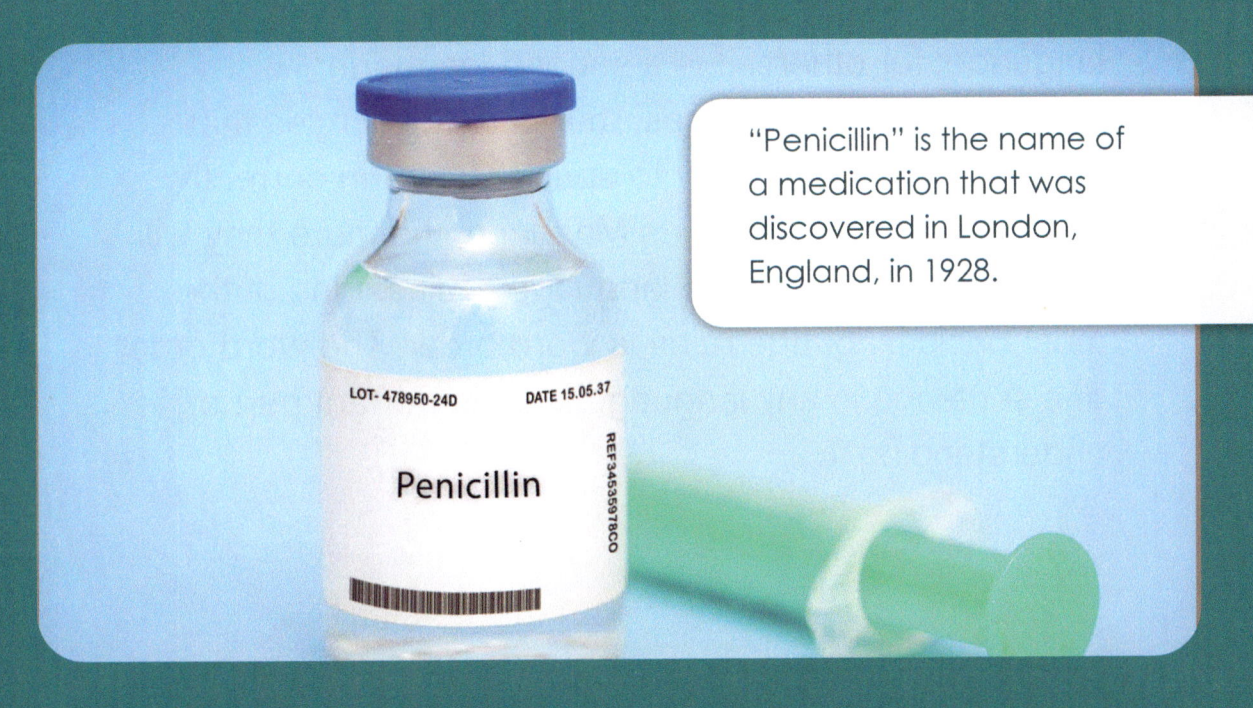

"Penicillin" is the name of a medication that was discovered in London, England, in 1928.

Mandarin

Mandarin is by far the most widely spoken Chinese language. It is considered the lingua franca of China. This phrase describes a language that is commonly spoken by people with different native languages. For example, English is a lingua franca for much of the world; it is taught in schools in almost every country. Within China, Mandarin is spoken by much of the population. For some, it is a native language; for others, it is a second language.

> Mandarin is most commonly written in simplified Chinese.

As with all languages, there are many rules that a person needs to follow to speak Mandarin correctly. The more a person studies Mandarin, the more they will become familiar with the language's rules. One of the most basic language rules is word order. The word order of a sentence in any language is an important part of understanding it.

In some places in China, especially big cities, signs are written in both Chinese and English.

禁止進入

NO Entry

A mandarin is also a type of orange. It was not named after the language, but it is considered a lucky fruit in China. This is because the Chinese word for "orange" sounds like the word "wealth." Its color is also associated with gold.

The different forms of Chinese are sometimes called dialects, but in reality, they are completely different languages. Two dialects of the same language are mutually intelligible, or able to be understood by both people. Chinese languages are mutually unintelligible in some cases.

In Mandarin, as in English, basic sentences go in this order: subject, verb, object. An example in English is "I like sports." The sentence does not make much sense when it is said "Sports like I." However, Mandarin differs from English in several key ways. In English, a word that describes a period of time can be placed in almost any part of a sentence. "Today I'm going to the store," "I'm going to the store today," and "I'm going today to the store" all make sense. In Mandarin, time words are almost always placed right after the subject of the sentence. A word describing a place also has a specific spot in a sentence: before the verb, but after the time word. For example, the English sentence "He was born in 2002 in Beijing" becomes "He 2002 Beijing born in" in Mandarin.

Cantonese

Cantonese is China's other major dialect. It is mostly spoken in Hong Kong, Macao, and in provinces such as Guangdong and Guangxi. In fact, the dialect's name comes from Guangdong, which used to be called "Canton" by Europeans who had trouble pronouncing the province's real name. Cantonese is also spoken by many Chinese living in Europe and North America. This is because most people who moved out of China in the 20th century came from Cantonese-speaking areas.

Cantonese is most commonly written in traditional Chinese. Cantonese also has more than one Latinization system. Two of the most commonly used, which are called Cantonese pinyin and jyutping, attach numbers to each word to show which tone should be used.

Cantonese is generally considered harder to learn than Mandarin. One reason for this is that it has many more tones for a speaker to memorize and learn to say correctly. A common phrase used to describe Cantonese is that it has "nine sounds and six tones."

Three of the Cantonese tones, which are called "checked tones," are only used for words that end in p, t, or k. This means that, while these words are said in a different tone, the meaning of the word does not change based on that tone.

Guangdong's capital city, Guangzhou, is also sometimes called Canton.

Cantonese is the language
Hong Kong's government uses.

While Mandarin simply numbers its tones, Cantonese has names for all of its tones. The names of the six main tones are dark flat, dark rising, dark departing, light flat, light rising, and light departing. The three checked tones are upper dark entering, lower dark entering, and light entering.

Cantonese and Mandarin are mutually unintelligible. Each language tends to have different words for the same thing, and the different tones mean that even words that are the same in both languages tend to be pronounced very differently.

Most people who learn Chinese choose to study either Mandarin or Cantonese. When choosing between them, it's important for the student to think about when and where they will most often use that language. For instance, will they be talking mostly to people from the Chinese mainland, or from Hong Kong? Will they be spending a lot of time in China, or do they want to learn how to talk to the owner of their favorite Chinese restaurant in Ohio?

Other Languages

Although Mandarin and Cantonese are by far the most popular of the Chinese languages, there are many other languages as well. Due to differences in vocabulary and pronunciation, these languages are mutually unintelligible to each other and to Mandarin and Cantonese. Below is a short overview of just a few of them.

Other Chinese languages include Yue, Jin, Jiangxi, Xiang, and Bai. Although China has been a unified country since 221 BCE, Mandarin was not made the official language until 1909. Until that time, different parts of China kept speaking their own unique languages.

- Wu is a language group that includes several different dialects. It's mainly spoken in Shanghai. About 8 percent of Chinese people speak Wu. Although that may sound like a small number, it translates to about 85 million people. Wu has seven or eight tones. It also uses a way of making sounds with the throat that has fallen out of use in Mandarin.

The city of Shanghai is one of very few places where Wu is spoken.

The Chinese written language is still the same and can unite all Chinese speakers, no matter which Chinese language they speak.

Han Chinese are the majority ethnic group in China. Each minority group has its own language, but many do not have a written system to go along with it. This is part of how *hanzi* became so popular throughout the country, even among people who do not speak Mandarin.

- Min is another language group. Experts disagree on how many languages make up the Min group. Some say there are two, some say five, and a few break it down into as many as nine. Min speakers use the same written Chinese language as other Chinese speakers, but they have their own way of pronouncing the words. This unique pronunciation is called Tang Min.

- Hakka is the language of the Hakka ethnic group, but not every Hakka person speaks the language. The best-known dialect of Hakka is spoken in Guangdong, so it is very similar to Cantonese; it uses many of the same words and tones as Cantonese, but its vowel sounds are closer to Mandarin. Hakka is also so similar to the Gan language that they are sometimes grouped into one, called Gan-Hakka.

Hard to Learn

Chinese is very hard for English speakers to learn, and English is hard for Chinese speakers to learn. Of course, the most obvious difference between the two is the tones. A Chinese speaker may have trouble figuring out what an English speaker is trying to say, even if they understand all the words. This is

Chinese speakers who are learning English also tend to have trouble with English tenses. Because Chinese uses time words instead of verb tenses, there is no such thing as past or present tense in Chinese. This is why a Chinese speaker who is just starting to learn English may say everything in the present tense.

because a change in tone does not change the meaning of an English word, but it can change the meaning of an entire sentence. Similarly, an English speaker may find it hard at first to hear the differences between the tones. This can cause them to get homophones confused.

Although learning Chinese can be difficult for English speakers, many people feel proud of themselves once they master the language. Learning a difficult language with a long history is an amazing accomplishment!

People who are learning a new language start out with very simple words and move on to more complex sentences later.

Glossary

abstract Expressing a quality apart from an object.

complex Not easy to understand or explain, having many parts.

context The setting of a word or phrase in speaking or writing that determines or affects its meaning.

correspond To match or agree with.

dialect A form of language spoken in a certain area that uses some of its own words, grammar, and pronunciations.

font A style of lettering.

homophone A word that sounds the same as another but has a different meaning and often a different spelling.

imperial Having to do with an empire or emperor.

neutral Without pronounced characteristics.

unique One of a kind.

For More Information

Asia Society and Museum
725 Park Avenue
New York, NY 10021
(212) 288-6400
Website: asiasociety.org/
The Asia Society works to educate people about Asian cultures and countries through education, including the learning of Chinese languages.

Chinese Language Institute (CLI)
31 Chaoyang Xilu
Guilin, Guangxi, China 541004
(888) 781-8383
+86 0773-759-9367
Website: studycli.org/
This organization offers students of Chinese languages an immersive experience to gain fluency and understanding of culture.

Chinese Language Teachers Association, USA (CLTA)
c/o Department of Modern Languages, Literatures, and Linguistics
University of Oklahoma
780 Van Vleet Oval
Norman, OK 73019
Website: www.clta-us.org/
The CLTA is a professional organization focused on supporting educators of Chinese languages.

Institute for Chinese Studies
140 Enarson Classroom Building
2009 Millikin Road
Columbus, OH 43210
(614) 247-6893
Website: https://easc.osu.edu/ics
This institute within the Ohio State University is a hub for scholarly research, student training, and public education programs.

National Museum of China
16 E Chang'an Ave.
Dongcheng Qu, China
+86 10 6511 6400
Website: en.chnmuseum.cn
This well-regarded museum holds stunning examples of ancient calligraphy.

National Museum of Chinese Writing
656 Renmin Boulevard East Section
Beiguan district
Anyang, Henan, China
This museum is dedicated to the country's writing system, showcasing a collection of over 4,000 items representing the history of Chinese calligraphy as well as writing systems of ethnic minorities.

For Further Reading

Avrick, Rachel. *Chinese Character Practice Workbook for Kids: 100 Essential Chinese Characters Made Easy.* Emeryville, CA: Rockridge Press, 2021.

Greenwood, Elinor. *Get Talking Chinese: Mandarin Chinese for Beginners.* New York, NY: DK Publishing, 2021.

He, Zhihong, and Guillaume Olive. *My First Book of Chinese Calligraphy.* Tokyo, Japan: Tuttle Publishing, 2022.

Li, Jason, An Xiao Mina, and Jennifer 8. Lee. *The Hanmoji Handbook.* Somerville, MA: MITeen Press, 2022.

Young, Ed. *Voices of the Heart.* New York, NY: Seven Stories Press, 2019.

Bibliography

"Chinese Calligraphy, an Introduction." Khan Academy. Accessed on April 8, 2024. https://www.khanacademy.org/humanities/art-asia/imperial-china/beginners-guide-imperial-china/a/chinese-calligraphy-an-introduction.

"Chinese Speaking Countries." WorldData. February 2024. https://www.worlddata.info/languages/chinese.php.

"How Many Languages Are Spoken in China?" K & J Translations. January 12, 2020. https://www.kjtranslations.com/blog/how-many-languages-are-spoken-in-china/.

Lin, Kathy. *"Chinese Language."* EthnoMed. Accessed on April 8, 2024. https://ethnomed.org/resource/chinese-language/#.

Monroy, Marco. *"Why Isn't There a Chinese Alphabet? A Useful Language Guide."* Berlitz. November 22, 2022. https://www.berlitz.com/blog/chinese-alphabet.

Su, Qiu Gui. *"History of Mandarin Chinese."* ThoughtCo. June 14, 2019. https://www.thoughtco.com/introduction-to-mandarin-chinese-2278430.

"What Are Tonal Languages?" Universal Translation Services. October 28, 2022. https://www.universal-translation-services.com/what-are-tonal-languages/.

"Which Words Did English Take from Other Languages?" Dictionary.com. October 1, 2018. https://www.dictionary.com/e/borrowed-words/.

Xie, Sunny. *"The 7 Main Differences Between Mandarin and Cantonese."* China Highlights. March 30, 2024. https://www.chinahighlights.com/travelguide/chinese-language/cantonese-vs-mandarin.htm.

Yee, Chinag. *"Chinese Calligraphy."* Encyclopedia Britannica. Accessed on April 8, 2024. https://www.britannica.com/art/Chinese-calligraphy

Index